The Ethics of

Human Cloning

Neil G Messer

Tutor in Ethics, the Queen's Foundation, Birmingham
Ministerial Training Officer, West Midlands Synod, URC

GROVE BOOKS LIMITED
RIDLEY HALL RD CAMBRIDGE CB3 9HU

Contents

1. Introduction: A Brief History of Cloning 3

2. The Risk Business 9

3. Welcoming the Stranger 11

4. Photocopying our Souls? 16

5. Eden and Babel 19

6. Conclusions 22

Acknowledgements

I am grateful to the Grove Ethics Group for inviting me to write this booklet, and to Dr Dave Leal for his comments and suggestions on successive drafts. Heartfelt thanks also to my wife, Janet, for her support, encouragement and constructive criticism of my work, and to my children, Fiona and Rebecca, for reminding me that there is more to life than Christian Ethics.

The Cover Illustration is by Peter Ashton

First Impression July 2001
ISSN 1470-854X
ISBN 1 85174 470 3

1
Introduction: A Brief History of Cloning

In February 1997, a ewe named Dolly became the most famous sheep in the world. She was the first mammal to be cloned using a cell from an adult animal, though this achievement was just the latest in a long line of research in animal cloning.[1]

Cloning means producing a genetically identical copy of an animal or plant. All living things carry within them a genetic blueprint, almost always encoded in deoxyribonucleic acid (DNA), that contains the instructions which play a large part in determining that individual's physical characteristics.[2] In many-celled organisms, such as humans, each cell (with a few exceptions) carries a complete copy of the individual's genetic blueprint. Almost all the genetic material is found in the *nucleus*, a separate compartment within the cell which often appears as a dark body within the cell when it is examined under the microscope.

Because almost all of an individual's genetic information is encoded in the DNA contained within the nucleus, if two individuals have copies of the same nuclear DNA, they will be very nearly genetically identical. In other words, they will be *clones*. Cloning occurs widely in nature, and is used as a reproductive strategy by many plants and invertebrate animals. However, humans, in common with other mammals, do not use this strategy, but instead reproduce sexually. The nearest thing to cloning that takes place naturally in humans is the occasional and unpredictable occurrence of monozygotic (identical) twins. In twinning, the embryo splits at a very early stage into two, and each part continues to develop normally. The individuals that develop from the two parts of the split embryo share the same genetic blueprint, and are therefore genetically identical.

Artificial cloning has a longer history than is sometimes realized. The propagation of plants by taking cuttings is a form of cloning. However, the cloning of vertebrate animals is much more difficult. In the 1950s and '60s, John Gurdon and others succeeded in cloning various species of frog and toad by nuclear transfer,[3] but the cloning of mammals has only become possible in the last few years.

There are two main approaches to mammalian cloning, both illustrated in figure 1 (overleaf). Cloning by embryo splitting mimics the natural process of

---

1 I Wilmut *et al*, 'Viable Offspring Derived from Foetal and Adult Mammalian Cells,' *Nature*, Vol 385 (1997), pp 810–813.
2 For an account of the structure and function of DNA, see N G Messer, *Genes, Persons and God: Theological and Ethical Reflections on Human Genetic Manipulation* (Grove Ethical Studies booklet E 95).
3 P Ramsey, *Fabricated Man* (New Haven: Yale, 1970) pp 64–65, and references therein.

twinning. It relies on the fact that, very early in an embryo's development, each of its cells has the potential to develop into an embryo, and thence an individual, by itself: the cells are *totipotent*. This potential is gradually lost as the embryo develops, and each of its cells becomes specialized in a different way. But if the embryo is split into individual cells or small groups of cells at a stage when the cells are still totipotent, then each resulting cell or group of cells may develop into an individual that is genetically identical to the others that have developed from the same original embryo.

In cloning by nuclear transfer, the nucleus is removed from an unfertilized egg cell. Then a cell nucleus from the individual to be cloned is introduced into this enucleated egg cell. If this is done under the right conditions, the egg cell then begins to divide and go through the process of embryonic and foetal development as if it had been fertilized in the normal way.

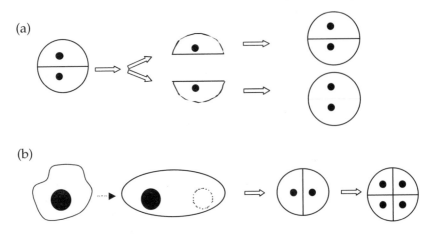

Figure 1. Approaches to mammalian cloning: (a) embryo splitting; (b) nuclear transfer

There were a number of experiments on mammalian cloning before Dolly, including the successful cloning of two sheep, Megan and Morag, by the researchers who later cloned Dolly.[4] Dolly, however, represented a new departure because she was the first mammal to have been cloned using a nucleus taken from an *adult* animal. This was a considerable technical challenge—indeed, there had been some doubt as to whether it would ever be possible. When Wilmut and his colleagues succeeded, this raised the possibility for the first time that an existing adult mammal (as opposed to an embryo) could be cloned. Since 1997, research-

---

4   K H S Campbell *et al*, 'Sheep Cloned by Nuclear Transfer from a Cultured Cell Line,' *Nature*, Vol 380 (1996), pp 64–66.

ers around the world have cloned other mammals, including mice and cows, by nuclear transfer.[5] No-one yet knows whether cloning by nuclear transfer will be possible in humans, though Wilmut, in evidence to the House of Commons Science and Technology Select Committee, said, 'It would be my belief that if you really wanted to do it, it could be done.'[6]

The Roslin Institute's work on cloning was in a sense a by-product of Wilmut's main aim. Wilmut and his colleagues had succeeded in genetically engineering sheep to produce a human protein, with important medical uses, in their milk. Cloning was a way of reliably reproducing sheep with the desired genetic change.[7] However, a number of other applications of animal cloning has been envisaged. It might allow pure research into the mechanisms of mammalian genetics. It might be possible to clone genetically modified mice which modelled various human diseases, thus allowing potential treatments to be tested on them. Pigs that had been genetically modified so that their organs were suitable for transplantation into humans could be cloned to increase the supply of such organs. Herds of genetically identical farm animals could be mass-produced by cloning. Most of these applications remain highly speculative, and may turn out to be technically impractical. They also raise a number of serious ethical issues.[8]

However, most of the ethical concern with cloning has been about the possible uses of the technology in humans. One use is *reproductive cloning*: generating a human child by cloning. The following are some of the reasons that have been suggested, with varying degrees of plausibility, for attempting this:

(i)   For some infertile couples, it would allow the possibility of having a child that had some biological relation to both of them and did not rely on donated eggs or sperm: most of the genetic material would come from the man, gestation would be in the woman's womb. In fact, in this scenario, a very small amount of genetic material *would* come from the woman, since the intracellular structures known as mitochondria contain a small amount of their own DNA, which is passed on from mother, but not father, to child during normal reproduction. A cloned child derived from the woman's enucleated egg and a nucleus from one of the man's cells would have the woman's mitochondrial DNA. It should be stressed, though, that this would be a tiny fraction of the total DNA in the cell, and would make very little difference to the phenotype (the observable characteristics) of the child.

(ii)   Some genetic diseases affect the mitochondrial, rather than the nuclear, DNA. Women carrying affected mitochondrial DNA cannot avoid passing these

5   D Solter, 'Dolly *is* a clone—and no longer alone,' *Nature*, Vol 394 (1998), p 315ff.
6   *The Baby Makers: Unnatural Practices* (Channel 4, 25 May 1999).
7   I Wilmut and D Bruce, 'Dolly Mixture,' in D Bruce and A Bruce (eds), *Engineering Genesis: The Ethics of Genetic Engineering in Non-Human Species* (London: Earthscan, 1998) pp 71–76.
8   *ibid*, chs 2 and 5; A Linzey, 'Ethical and Theological Objections to Animal Cloning,' *Bulletin of Medical Ethics*, No 131 (September 1997), pp 18–22.

genetic defects onto their children. Nuclear transfer technology might offer a way for such women to have children genetically related to them or their partners without passing on these genetic defects. A nucleus from the woman or her partner would be inserted in an enucleated egg cell from an unaffected donor, and the resulting embryonic clone implanted in the woman's womb.

(iii) Parents whose child had died could produce a clone from one of the dead child's cells.

(iv) A sick child, needing an organ or tissue transplant, might be cloned so that the clone could be a source of perfectly compatible organs or tissues for transplant.

(v) Prominent people, such as leading sports personalities, artists or politicians, might be cloned in the hope that their clones would be equally gifted and contribute as much to society.

(vi) People might seek to achieve a kind of immortality by cloning themselves. For example, the American scientist Richard Seed was widely reported as saying, soon after the news of Dolly's cloning, 'God intended for man to become one with God...Cloning and the reprogramming of DNA is the first serious step in becoming one with God.'[9]

(vii) Cloning might be used as a eugenic tool, perhaps with racist intent, a fear expressed by Peter J Paris: 'Since Europeans and Euro-Americans have never been able to affirm the value of the world's darker races as equals, there is little reason to believe that their scientists would not seek to rid the world of some of its racial diversity by combining the science of eugenics with that of human cloning.'[10]

A number of other applications of the technology are often referred to under the general heading of *therapeutic cloning*. These so-called 'therapeutic' applications make use of the fact that the cells of embryos are *pluripotent*—that is to say, they have the potential to give rise to any of the cells found in an adult. Such pluripotent cells are often known as *embryonic stem (ES) cells*. Possible future uses for cloned stem cells include the following:[11]

(i) If a patient needs a supply of cells or tissues for grafting (for example, to replace heart muscle, brain tissue or skin that has been damaged by accident or disease), a nucleus from one of his cells could be implanted into a donated egg cell to produce an embryo that could then be used as a source of stem cells. Animal research suggests that if stem cells are injected into a tissue or

9   D Sapsted and R Highfield, 'Plea for Cash to Clone Humans,' *Daily Telegraph*, 8 January 1998, pp 1–2.
10   P J Paris, 'A View from the Underside,' in R Cole-Turner (ed) *Human Cloning: Religious Responses* (Louisville: Westminster John Knox), p 47.
11   See Human Genetics Advisory Commission / Human Fertilization and Embryology Authority, *Cloning Issues in Reproduction, Science and Medicine* (London: HGAC, 1998), Nuffield Council on Bioethics, *Stem Cell Therapy: The Ethical Issues* (London: Nuffield Council, 2000) and L Donaldson (chair), *Stem Cell Research: Medical Progress With Responsibility* (London: Department of Health, 2000).

organ, they can become incorporated and function as a normal part of it.

(ii)   In a women carrying a mitochondrial disease, nuclear transfer technology could be used to create a hybrid egg cell containing a nucleus from one of her eggs but mitochondria from an unaffected donor, which could then be fertilized *in vitro*. This would not be the same as using reproductive cloning to avoid mitochondrial disease (as described earlier), since the embryo would result from the fertilization of an egg by a sperm cell, as in normal conception.

(iii)   Cloning could be used to create human embryos for research into fertility and reproduction, the mechanisms underlying cancer, ageing and other areas. Currently research on human embryos up to 14 days after fertilization is permissible in the UK under the terms of the Human Fertilization and Embryology Act (1990).

Many of these applications would involve the creation of a human embryo to be used in research or as a source of cells. The end result of either would be the destruction of the embryo. Therefore our moral assessment of these applications will depend to a large extent on our understanding of the moral status of the human embryo. If, for example, a human embryo is a person with the same moral status as an adult human being from the moment of conception, such uses of embryos will clearly be unacceptable. If, on the other hand, as the Warnock Report concluded, human embryos have a special status which is nonetheless not the same as that of a child or adult, such uses of embryos may be permissible.[12] It is worth noting that if we decline to take a position on the status of the embryo, this 'agnostic' attitude may commit us to a more restrictive attitude to its use than is often acknowledged; Oliver O'Donovan has made a similar point about the foetus in the context of the abortion debate.[13]

It has been suggested that it may be possible to make pluripotent human stem cells directly from adult cells without having to create embryos *en route*, drawing on the lessons learned from cloning. If this were the case, some of the above applications might be less ethically problematic. There is currently some controversy as to how likely this is, and whether it could be done without some initial research on embryonic stem cells. The UK Chief Medical Officer's Expert Group took the view that research on embryonic stem cells would be necessary first, and recommended that this should be permitted by law.[14] Early in 2001, Parliament extended the provisions of the Human Fertilization and Embryol-

---

12   M Warnock (Chairman), *Report of the Committee of Inquiry into Human Fertilization and Embryology* (London: HMSO, 1984).

13   O O'Donovan, *The Christian and the Unborn Child* (Grove Ethics booklet E 1) p 5. It is also worth noting that claims such as the ones represented here about the status of the foetus often depend on criteria of personhood or moral worth (such as rationality or sentience). Such 'criterial' arguments about personhood will be called into question in chapter 4. I am grateful to Dr Dave Leal for clarifying this point.

14   Donaldson, *Stem Cell Research*, paras 2.11–2.14, 5.10.

ogy Act to make such research possible; human reproductive cloning remains illegal in the UK.[15]

From this wide range of issues, the present discussion will focus on human reproductive cloning. A discussion of therapeutic cloning, important though it is, is beyond the scope of this booklet. Among the issues discussed will be: (i) the possible consequences of human cloning, both for the individuals concerned and for the wider society; (ii) the importance for human cloning of the distinction identified by O'Donovan between 'begetting' and 'making';[16] (iii) the implications of cloning for human individuality and personal identity; (iv) the proper scope and limits of our manipulation of the created world, including ourselves and each other; and (v) the roles that Christians might play in public debate and policy-making on matters such as human cloning.

15 *Hansard (House of Commons Daily Debates)* 19 December 2000, col 266; *Hansard (House of Lords Debates)* 22 January 2001, col 124.
16 O M T O'Donovan, *Begotten or Made?* (Oxford: Clarendon, 1984).

2

The Risk Business

Much, though not all, of the public discussion of human cloning has focused on risk of harm to the individual. In the work of Ian Wilmut's team, Dolly was the only one of 277 attempted clones that developed into a healthy adult. Many others were lost during pregnancy, were still-born or suffered severe birth defects.[17] It is widely agreed that it would be unacceptable to attempt human cloning with those odds, but what if the odds could be shortened until the risks were no greater than those of a natural conception and pregnancy (always assuming we have any reliable estimate of the latter)?

One point not often acknowledged in this discussion is that, though it might be possible to estimate the risks in advance, we could not know for certain what the level of risk in human cloning was until we tried it. Experiments on other animals might give some idea of the risks, but would not give unequivocal answers about the risks in humans, since the embryology of every mammal is different. Therefore the first clones would in a sense inevitably be 'experimental subjects,' and, in the nature of the case, the experiment would be without their consent. Paul Ramsey made a similar observation about the birth in 1978 of Louise Brown, the first IVF baby, arguing that it was wrong in principle to develop IVF, because it inevitably exposed children to some risk, however slight, that was not for their direct benefit and to which they could not give their consent.[18] This argument in itself, though, may not be decisive against reproductive technologies, or indeed against human cloning. For one thing, risk may not always be as neatly quantifiable as Ramsey's argument seems to require, particularly in the area of human procreation. For another, the only alternatives as far as Louise Brown was concerned were to be born as a result of IVF or never to exist—so it may not be straightforward to say in what sense she was exposed to risk by virtue of being conceived by IVF.[19]

But there are also wider-ranging questions about consequences than individual risks and benefits. A key question to ask about any new technology is: *For whose benefit, and at whose cost, is this being done?* Who stands to gain from human cloning. Who stands to lose out?

It might seem as if some very vulnerable individuals and groups would benefit. For example, cloning might enable some people to have children who could

17   I Wilmut *et al*, *Nature*, Vol 385 (1997), pp 810–813.
18   P Ramsey, 'On In Vitro Fertilization,' reprinted in S E Lammers and A Verhey (eds), *On Moral Medicine: Theological Voices in Medical Ethics* (Grand Rapids: Eerdmans, 1st ed, 1987) pp 339–345.
19   For two views of these questions, see N J Zohar, 'Prospects for "Genetic Therapy"—Can a Person Benefit from Being Altered?' *Bioethics*, Vol 5.4 (1991), pp 275–288, and J P Kahn, 'Genetic Harm: Bitten by the Body that Keeps You?' *Bioethics*, Vol 5.4 (1991), pp 289–308.

not do so by any other means. One such case is that of Victoria Oldaker. She was born without ovaries or a uterus, and so could not benefit from any current technique in reproductive medicine. Interviewed during the 1999 Channel 4 series *The Baby Makers*, she said: 'I have always wanted a child, and I will do anything to get one, and if that means being the first person ever to have a cloned child, and to live with that, then that's what I will do…if it's your only option, your only chance, you'll do anything to do it.'[20]

But it may not be as simple as this. In-vitro fertilization (IVF) is a procedure which also appears to offer enormous benefit to vulnerable people, particularly couples who long to have children, but suffer the pain and loss of infertility. Yet the experience of those who undergo IVF suggests that the benefits are two-edged. There is considerable psychological and indeed physical cost to going through procedures that can be intrusive, painful and by no means risk-free, particularly for the woman, and on which an enormous amount is staked emotionally but with a very uncertain prospect of success.[21] Furthermore, some feminist critics of IVF argue that it is at best ambiguously beneficial, and at worst positively harmful, to women's interests. For example, it entails intrusive investigation into women's sexual and reproductive lives, and can be a way in which women's bodies are instrumentalized by a patriarchal culture.[22] Such critiques of IVF are by no means common ground among feminists (or others), but I cite them to illustrate that a reproductive technology may be at best a mixed blessing to those whom it would appear at first sight to benefit.

Peter J Paris has voiced concerns about a number of possible ways in which the effects of human cloning could be harmful to the interests of minority ethnic groups.[23] For example, I cited in chapter 1 his concern that cloning could be used in a racist eugenic programme. It seems relatively unlikely that cloning by itself would ever become widespread enough to be a serious eugenic tool, though it is probably unwise to say confidently that it could *never* happen. However, it is more plausible that its use as one of a battery of reproductive techniques might lead gradually to a widespread expectation of the 'quality control' of children which, as well as being theologically and ethically objectionable in other ways, could turn out to be highly discriminatory. I shall return to this concern in the next chapter.

---

20 *The Baby Makers: Unnatural Practices*, Channel 4, 25th May 1999.
21 A Dyson, *The Ethics of IVF* (London: Mowbray, 1995) ch 4.
22 *ibid*, ch 5.
23 Paris, in Cole-Turner (ed) *Human Cloning*, pp 43–48.

3

Welcoming the Stranger

Oliver O'Donovan has argued that there is a crucial distinction between those whom we *beget* and that which we *make*.[24] Those whom we beget are like us and can be in a relationship of equals with us. That which we make, by contrast, is in a sense alienated from us—product rather than progeny, so to speak. On this basis, O'Donovan develops a general critique of the new reproductive technologies, that they tend to introduce an element of 'making' into the process of human 'begetting' or procreation. One of the things which distinguish 'begetting' from 'making,' he holds, is the contingency and chanciness of the former—it is never fully under our control, so we can never see our children as things designed and made by us. Stanley Hauerwas has made a similar point—that, contrary to our usual intuitions, we do not choose to have children, but rather are called to receive them as gifts.

> [Children] are basic and perhaps the most essential gifts that we have because they teach us how to be. That is, they create in us the proper need to want to love and regard another. For love born of need is always manipulative love unless it is based on the regard of the other as an entity that is not in my control but who is all the more valuable because I do not control him. Children are gifts exactly because they draw our love to them while refusing to be as we wish them to be.[25]

But if we develop techniques for selecting and controlling our children's genotype, we are in effect attempting to introduce an element of 'making' into our procreation. It could then become all too easy to see a child as an artefact or a commodity rather than an Other whom I have to respect as she is, in all her stubborn otherness.

A common Christian objection to reproductive cloning is that it would undermine this attitude of welcoming the stranger by exerting total control over the genotype of the child. In O'Donovan's terms, the child would to a very significant extent be 'made' rather than 'begotten.' This objection is advanced, for example, by Donald Bruce:

> By definition, to clone is to exercise unprecedented control over the genetic dimension of another individual...Such control by one human over another

---

24 O'Donovan, *Begotten or Made?*, p 1 and passim.
25 S Hauerwas, *Truthfulness and Tragedy: Further investigations into Christian Ethics* (Notre Dame: University of Notre Dame Press, 1977) p 153.

is incompatible with the ethical notion of human freedom...that each individual's genetic identity should be inherently unpredictable and unplanned.[26]

In similar vein, Peter Paris worries that it will be too easy for us to regard human clones as less than fully human:

> [It] is conceivable that humans would be capable of defining human clones as quasihuman because they are derived from an original and produced by human technology in lieu of natural processes...It is because we regard them as less than human that we justify human domination of livestock and the making of them into mere objects of utility. Who is to say that human clones might not be treated similarly?[27]

However, the 'cloning as control' objection is often stated in a rather vague manner, in which several different concerns may be woven together. It may be helpful to separate different versions of it:

(i) *Anyone who seeks to clone a child from themselves is consciously attempting to exercise this control or commodification of children.* This is demonstrably false. For example, for some individuals or couples, cloning would represent the only possibility of having a child that is biologically 'theirs.' For such people, the motivation for cloning appears to have little to do with exercising control over the child's phenotype or development, and much more to do with the natural and widespread human desire to have children. This in turn raises other serious questions (for example: to what lengths, beyond natural conception, are we entitled to go in order to satisfy this desire?) but it does suggest that this version of the 'control' objection is an insecure argument. It will always be vulnerable to contradiction by would-be parents for whom cloning is, as it were, a by-product of the simple desire to have children.

(ii) *Reproductive cloning opens up new possibilities of control and commodification.* A society might give a limited permission for it, perhaps in the first instance as a last-resort response to infertility, while attempting to guard against the wholesale control and commodification of children that objectors fear. But this limited permission, over the course of time, might bring about a gradual change in attitudes such that it became normal to control the genotype of one's children, and was perhaps even considered irresponsible not to. This would be a case of what Robin Gill has called 'procedural deterioration.' He gives the example of UK abortion law, where what started as an exceptional permission has become a normal expectation.[28] It may be difficult to demon-

26 D Bruce, 'Should We Clone Humans?' Church of Scotland Society, Religion and Technology Project website, http://www.srtp.org.uk/clonhum2.htm (19 November 1998).
27 Paris, *op cit*, p 46.
28 R Gill, 'The Challenge of Euthanasia,' in R Gill (ed), *Euthanasia and the Churches* (London: Cassell, 1998) pp 37–38.

strate in advance that this kind of 'procedural deterioration' *would* occur, but the risk of it would at least argue for being *very* cautious before allowing reproductive cloning. A warning sign may be detected in the words of Roger Gosden, a researcher in reproductive medicine, during the Channel 4 *Baby Makers* documentary cited earlier:

> The closing decades of the twentieth century have been ones where we've been pre-occupied in reproductive science with trying to overcome problems of infertility…In the twenty-first century, I believe that we'll be emphasizing much more the quality of those children, so that people can have a healthy child at the time they want, and perhaps with other characteristics that they seek.[29]

Gosden's comments were presented in the context of a discussion of IVF and pre-implantation genetic diagnosis rather than cloning, but it is not difficult to see cloning as part of the battery of techniques, also including genetic manipulation, IVF and genetic diagnostic techniques, that taken together could both make such quality control possible and lead people to expect it. It can be argued that such an expectation of quality control would tend to contradict our understanding, as Hauerwas puts it, of children as gifts whom we are called to receive and welcome as they are. This need not mean that individual parents would be incapable of loving or caring for their cloned or genetically enhanced children, but it might suggest the risk of a general and very far-reaching shift in attitudes to children.

(iii) *The control of children's genotypes could be practised in discriminatory ways*—a concern related to the arguments of Peter Paris cited in chapter 2. If there were a process of procedural deterioration which led to a widespread expectation that parents could use cloning, genetic manipulation and a range of other techniques to exercise quality control over their children, this would raise the further profound question of how 'quality' was understood. Gosden's words imply two criteria: 'a healthy child…perhaps with other characteristics that [the parents] seek.' Even the first, which sounds clear enough, is problematic. The meanings of 'health' and 'disease' are far from obvious, so it is by no means clear that all parents and their doctors would understand the same by 'a healthy child.'[30] His second criterion, 'other characteristics that they seek,' seems to be quite an open-ended invitation for parents to choose whatever they find desirable in a child and do whatever the technology allows to incorporate such characteristics into their progeny. Quite apart from other theological and ethical objections to such a project, if it were ever to become a realistic prospect, there would be a real risk that it

---

29 Channel 4, 25th May 1999.
30 See K Boyd, 'Disease, illness, sickness, health, healing and wholeness: exploring some elusive concepts' *Journal of Medical Ethics: Medical Humanities*, Vol 26 (2000), pp 9–17 for a recent discussion.

could reinforce and perpetuate selective images of desirable human beings. This could, like earlier exercises in eugenics, lend support to old prejudices; it could also foster new ones which cut across existing social divisions.[31]

(iv) *Cloning would undermine the meaning of procreation, regardless of the motives of individual parents.* Such an argument is developed by Brent Waters. Highly critical of the modern principle of 'procreative liberty' as a framework for thinking about reproduction, he prefers to place the discussion within a normative framework of 'familial integrity' drawn from an ideal pattern in which

> a genetically unrelated wife and husband [produce] children who are genetically related to each other and to both of their parents. It is this ordering of natural and social affinity which gives procreation its full meaning; collapsing either dimension deprives the roles of spouse, parent, child and sibling of their complete and mutual significance. The family also provides a place of unconditional belonging. Children are not routinely interviewed and invited to join a family, nor are they acquired as an accoutrement to an already established relationship. Rather, they grow out of an enlarging relationship to which they in turn contribute in establishing a family.[32]

For Waters, the 'meaning' of reproduction is to be found in this structure of roles and relationships, which provides the space in which familial love can flourish and grow. Cloning, in common with other more familiar attempts at the technological control of reproduction, disrupts this structure and '[voids] procreation of its meaning'; it is 'an exquisite parody of the one-flesh foundation of procreation, for it is one more step in reducing its purpose to whatever we will or choose it to be.'[33] He does not deny that parents could be capable of caring for their clones. However, he argues that cloning by its nature would nonetheless undermine family structures that support the unconditional acceptance of children, and instead would reinforce the view of reproduction as an exercise of parental will, subject to unfettered freedom of choice.

His argument would be stronger if he justified rather than assumed the shape of his 'framework of familial integrity,' and addressed, however briefly, the major questions that it raises.[34] For example, he does not comment on the status of adopted children and step-children, some of whom might seem to have been, in a sense, 'invited to join a family': are adoptive parenthood and

---

31 This point is made effectively by Andrew Niccol's film *Gattaca* (Columbia, 1997), which depicts a society that places strong pressure on parents to control the genetic health and quality of their children (albeit by IVF and pre-implantation diagnosis rather than cloning). In this dystopia, members both of the genetic élite (the 'valids') and of the underclass (the 'invalids') may be male or female, black or white.

32 B Waters, 'One Flesh? Cloning, Procreation and the Family,' in Cole-Turner (ed) *Human Cloning* p 83.

33 *ibid*, p 85.

34 For a brief survey of the questions, see S C Barton (ed), *The Family in Theological Perspective* (Edinburgh: T & T Clark, 1996) pp xi–xx; the papers collected in that volume discuss them in considerable depth.

step-parenthood to be viewed as lapses from the ideal, or in some other way? Nonetheless, Waters alerts us to the important possibility that there is, as it were, a moral structure to human parenthood that is jeopardized by the practice of cloning, whatever the motives of the individual practitioners.

In summary, then, 'control' arguments are unconvincing if they assert that everyone who sought to clone a child would necessarily be seeking to control and commodify that child, and consciously refusing to receive her as a gift (though this may well be true of some). But it is more convincing to argue, firstly, that control rather than unconditional acceptance is *implicit* in the act of cloning, and secondly, that its acceptance and use could lead gradually to a shift in attitudes and actions away from the unconditional acceptance of children and towards their control and commodification.

4
Photocopying our Souls?

A number of the essays in the volume edited by Ronald Cole-Turner make reference to a 1997 *Time* magazine article in which the question is asked, 'Can souls be Xeroxed?'[35] The use of such language by a mass-circulation weekly magazine is suggestive of a widespread suspicion that, in cloning a human being, we may be copying not only a genotype, but also the essence of a person's identity. (It is also interesting that apparently theological language is used by a secular publication to express the question; I shall return to this point in chapter 6). This suspicion is sometimes used as the basis of an ethical objection to reproductive cloning—that by making a genetic copy of a human individual, it somehow compromises the uniqueness and human dignity of both the 'parent' and the clone.[36] In what do personhood, personal identity and individuality consist, and what might be compromised to what extent by cloning?

It is universally acknowledged that genes alone do not determine an individual's physical or other characteristics. An individual's phenotype—the sum total of her observable characteristics—is the product of a complex interplay between her genotype (her 'genetic blueprint') and her environment from the early stages of embryonic development onwards. Even identical twins, who have identical genotypes, are not truly physically identical. For example, they have different fingerprints, thought to be the result of subtle differences in each twin's environment in the mother's womb during foetal development. Ronald Cole-Turner quotes psychological studies of identical twins which suggest that genetic factors define a range of possibilities for a person's behavioural and psychological traits, but that within this range of possibilities, her environment exercises a very significant influence.[37]

But at a deeper level, as the language of 'Xeroxing souls' implies, the question 'What constitutes personhood, personal identity and individuality?' is a *theological* question, which has had a long and complex history in Christian thought.[38] One highly significant recent development in theological anthropology has been the recovery of so-called 'relational' understandings of human personhood and identity, themselves springing from the recent flourishing of

35   J Kluger, 'Will we Follow the Sheep?' *Time*, March 10, 1997, pp 67–73; cited in Cole-Turner, *Human Cloning* eg in essays by T Peters (pp 12–24) and R Cole-Turner (pp 119–130).
36   There is an element of this objection in D Bruce, 'Should We Clone Humans?' (*op cit*, note 26), though he qualifies this by saying that he is more concerned about control than about genetic identity *per se*.
37   R Cole-Turner, 'At the Beginning,' in Cole-Turner, *op cit*, pp 122-124.
38   For a careful and comprehensive review, see S Rudman, *Concepts of the Person and Christian Ethics* (Cambridge: CUP, 1997). I have previously discussed personhood and its importance for human cloning in N G Messer, 'Human Cloning and Genetic Manipulation: Some Theological and Ethical Issues,' *Studies in Christian Ethics*, Vol 12.2 (1999), pp 1–16.

Trinitarian theology exemplified by John Zizioulas and Colin Gunton, among many others.[39] One example of such a theory of human personhood is that of Alistair McFadyen.[40] He explores what it means to be made in the image of God, describing 'vertical' and 'horizontal' dimensions of the image. The 'vertical' dimension is that human beings are created for relationship with God, a relationship which is 'structured from God's side as dialogue' (p 19). That is to say, God addresses us in a way which leaves us free either to respond with gratitude and praise, or to refuse such response. Insofar as we respond to God in such a way, our life 'has an undistorted structure' (p 19), but distortion is introduced into our life when we refuse the dialogue to which God invites us. Such undistorted or distorted forms of relationship with God constitute, over time, a 'history of communication' whose 'sedimentation' forms our personal identity (p 23 and chapter 3).

God's relationship of dialogue with us also calls for our response in the 'horizontal' dimension, that is to say, in our interpersonal and social relationships. Here, McFadyen draws on Jürgen Moltmann's Trinitarian theology to argue that the image of God in human beings must be understood in relational terms:

> Just as the Persons of the Trinity receive and maintain their identities through relation, and relations of a certain quality, then so would human persons only receive and maintain their identities through relations with others and would stand fully in God's image whenever these identities and relations achieved a certain quality (p 31).

By analogy with the relationships between the persons of the Trinity and the 'vertical' divine-human relationship, McFadyen argues that human relations which fully reflect God's image are *dialogical*, leaving the other free and uncoerced, and *'ex-centric,'* that is to say outward-looking and centred on the other rather than on oneself (pp 31–39). Like the vertical relationship with God, our relationships with one another in the horizontal dimension contribute to that sedimentation of communications which shapes our personal identity. Patterns of communication which are distorted by being in some measure coercive, self-centred and so on (in other words, sinful) cause our identity to develop in distorted ways, thereby limiting our freedom to relate to others in undistorted ways. Social structures as well as individual relationships can be distorted. In this fallen world, we are all born into such distorted patterns and structures, and in this sense are the inheritors of original sin. In such a world, God offers the possibility of redemption through Christ, which McFadyen discusses in terms of Jesus' call of the disciples. The call of Christ comes to us as perfectly undistorted communication (dialogical not coercive, other-centred not self-centred). The call invites *us* to respond in an undistorted way: 'Follow me' is an invitation to shift

---

39 J D Zizioulas, *Being as Communion: Studies in Personhood and the Church* (London: DLT, 1985); C E Gunton, *The Promise of Trinitarian Theology* (Edinburgh: T & T Clark, 2nd ed, 1997).

40 A I McFadyen, *The Call to Personhood: A Christian Theory of the Individual in Social Relationships* (Cambridge: CUP, 1990). Numbers in brackets in this and the following paragraphs refer to pages of this work.

the central focus of our lives from ourselves to Christ and others (pp 48–58). For McFadyen, as for Zizioulas, this experience is in some sense made real in the church, where the presence of Christ is experienced (pp 61–63).[41] The energy of the Holy Spirit is available to those who respond to Christ's call, holding out the possibility of living in transformed ways in this still-distorted world (pp 63–65).

If anything like McFadyen's theory is correct, then there is a great deal more to personal identity than genotype. Even in the horizontal dimension, our identity is shaped by the history of our relations with one another. There is of course a physical basis to this history. Every aspect of our communication with one another relies on the fact that we are embodied beings, and even our memory of relationships and events presumably has a basis in the microscopic detail of the neuronal connections within our brains. Our physical (including neurological) characteristics are of course influenced by our genes, but even at this level genetics exercises much less than total control. If McFadyen is right, our genes may set some parameters and constraints on the development of our identities, but a great deal more depends on our biographies.

But the prior 'call to personhood' is in the vertical dimension. It is God's address to us which first constitutes us as persons and, as it were, underwrites our identity. This suggests that the possibility of copying a *person* by cloning is remote, not only for the psychological and anthropological reasons advanced by Cole-Turner, but more fundamentally for the theological reason that our personhood and identity are God's gracious gift, not something that humans can manufacture or copy. We are, of course, called to play a part in the origins of persons—the limited but vital part known as *pro*creation. But procreation is not the same thing as creation.

So it is most unlikely that we would ever *succeed* in 'photocopying a soul.' However, there is a moral argument to be had, not just about what we succeed in doing, but also about what we should or should not *try* to do. Is it true to say that we are trying to 'photocopy a soul' or replicate a person's identity if we attempt reproductive cloning? Of the scenarios described in chapter 1, some do not seem to answer directly to this description—for example, the childless couple who just want a child, and for whom the fact that she is a clone is incidental to their conscious intentions. However, others, such as the attempt to replace a lost child, copy oneself or copy a famous or gifted individual, look much more like attempts to replicate a personal identity—to 'photocopy a soul.' It is also worth noting that if the argument of chapter 3 is correct, then regardless of the conscious and explicit intentions of the would-be cloners, there is a kind of control *implicit* in the practice of cloning that is the very opposite of the undistorted, non-coercive and other-centred relationships to which God's call to personhood invites us. We now turn to the question of the theological and ethical significance of *attempting* to 'photocopy a soul.'

41   Zizioulas, *Being as Communion*, pp 18–20.

5

Eden and Babel

In Genesis 2, God places Adam in the garden of Eden, commands him to take care of it and brings the animals to him to be named: in other words, human beings are entrusted by God with the care of the created order, and given the authority by God to discharge that trust. But in Genesis 11, we find human beings over-reaching themselves, using God-given skill and ingenuity to try and reach up to heaven, to make a name for themselves, in effect to become like gods—forgetting that they are *creatures* of the true God.

These two stories illustrate a tension inherent in our calling from God. On the one hand, we are finite and limited creatures, not infinite and all-powerful creators. We are mortals rather than God, and it is both foolish and self-destructive for us to forget it. But on the other hand, God has given us the ability to push back our limits—to take some measure of control and authority over the created order, and to share in God's creative work. And so this pair of stories illustrates two opposite dangers: on the one hand, an abdication of our responsibility in and for the created order, and a fatalistic refusal to put our God-given skill and ingenuity to good use; on the other, the arrogant use of that skill and ingenuity to pretend that we have no limits—that we are gods.

Some Christians have seen cloning as a pretentious attempt to become like God. Paul Ramsey, foreseeing the possibility of human cloning as long ago as the 1960s, famously commented that 'Men ought not to play God until they have learned to be men, and after they have learned to be men they will not play God.'[42] Others have seen it as a legitimate part of our human calling. Joseph Fletcher, responding to Ramsey, wrote that 'The future is not to be sought in the stars but in us, in human beings. We don't pray for rain, we irrigate and seed clouds; we don't pray for cures, we rely on medicine…This is the direction of the biological revolution—that we turn more and more from creatures to creators.'[43] So which is right? How can we steer a proper course between the opposite dangers of passive fatalism and god-like pretension? And does reproductive cloning lie on this course or off it?

Elsewhere I have suggested that a helpful guide can be found in Dietrich Bonhoeffer's distinction between the ultimate and the penultimate.[44] The *ultimate*

42 Ramsey, *Fabricated Man*, p 138.
43 J Fletcher, *The Ethics of Genetic Control: Ending Reproductive Roulette* (Garden City, NY: Doubleday, 1974) p 200; quoted in Cole-Turner (ed) *Human Cloning*, p xii.
44 D Bonhoeffer, *Ethics* (ed E Bethge, trans N H Smith, London: Collins, 1964) pp 120–143. Numbers in brackets in this and the following paragraphs refer to pages of this work. For my earlier use of Bonhoeffer's categories, see Messer, 'Human Cloning and Genetic Manipulation' pp 10–14.

is 'The word of the justifying grace of God' (p 125), God's final word to us in Christ, which brings us salvation and new life. The *penultimate* things are those this-worldly things which come before God's word of justification. The ultimate 'entirely annuls and invalidates' the penultimate (p 125), because the penultimate cannot save or justify us. Yet the penultimate is also essential, because it is the realm through which people must pass before they can hear God's justifying word: 'for the sake of the ultimate, the penultimate must be preserved' (p 134).

The ultimate is God's task, not ours. Only God in Christ can bring us to receive divine forgiveness and salvation. But the penultimate *is* our task. We have a responsibility to create this-worldly conditions which can prepare the way for people to receive God's grace.

> The hungry man needs bread and the homeless man a roof; the dispossessed need justice and the lonely need fellowship; the undisciplined need order and the slave needs freedom...If the hungry man does not attain to faith, then the guilt falls on those who refused him bread. To provide the hungry man with bread is to prepare the way for the coming of grace. (p 137)

Science, technology and medicine, like other human activities, can have a God-given *penultimate* role—to remove the obstacles and prepare the way for the coming of God's grace. If this is indeed where the theological mandate for such activities is to be found, it suggests a theological criterion by which they may be judged adequate or found wanting. They are rightly used if, and only if, they do indeed serve to '[prepare] the way for the word' (p 135), rather than placing obstacles in its way. If we try to use science, technology and medicine to accomplish *ultimate* tasks, we are attempting to take upon ourselves something that only God can do—in effect, pretending that we are gods. Like the builders of the tower of Babel, we thereby alienate ourselves *from* God, who is the true source of our life and hope. For example, if we tried to use genetic engineering to make people less violent and more caring, we would be trying to solve what are really moral and spiritual problems by technological means. This could all too easily lead us to think that we could, as it were, save ourselves by a technological fix.

In my view, reproductive cloning cannot be justified by Bonhoeffer's theological mandate. Some cloning scenarios, I claimed in chapter 4, are overt attempts to determine the identity of the person brought into being by cloning—to 'Xerox a soul' in the language of *Time* magazine. This would be true of the attempt to replace a dead child, to copy oneself or to copy a famous and gifted individual. If we do this, we are in effect trying to become *creators*, refusing the limitations and contingencies of *procreation*. We are stating that we are no longer willing to receive our children, whatever they are like, as God's gift. Joseph Fletcher, quoted at the beginning of this chapter, understood this very clearly and welcomed such a development. However, in the light of Bonhoeffer's distinction between the ultimate and the penultimate, it should be resisted, not welcomed, because the attempt to become creators is to try and take upon our-selves an ultimate task, one that is properly God's alone.[45]

What of the more apparently innocent uses of reproductive cloning, such as its use by infertile couples in an attempt to have children? The conscious moti-vation of such people is less likely to have anything to do with ultimate tasks or the attempt of creatures to become creators than in the scenarios mentioned in the previous paragraph. However, in chapter 3 I noted arguments that there is a kind of 'implicit meaning' of reproductive cloning that has to do with attempt-ing to control the development of a person's identity. If this is true, then not only the obviously grandiose and pretentious cloning scenarios, but also the appar-ently innocent ones and those that command our sympathy, may be attempts to do what is not properly ours, but God's to do.

---

45 It may seem strange to describe creation as an 'ultimate' task, when Bonhoeffer's use of this category has to do with God's redemptive and eschatological activity. However, I believe it can properly be so described. Bonhoeffer himself seems to resist a sharp separation between creation and redemption by insisting on the NT affirmation that 'the world…is created through Christ and with Christ as its end, and consists in Christ alone'; *Ethics*, pp 207–213; J Burtness, *Shaping the Future: The Ethics of Dietrich Bonhoeffer* (Philadelphia: Fortress, 1985) pp 83–85.

6

Conclusions

Many public policy discussions about bioethical issues seem to take place within a purely consequentialist framework—they exclude moral arguments other than those concerned with outcomes (such as attempts to weigh up the likely risks against benefits).[46] If the discussion of human reproductive cloning were limited to such a framework, we should probably conclude that we ought to be very cautious about permitting it, but that it may be justifiable in some circumstances. In effect, my argument in this booklet has been that there is more to be said than this. Firstly, there is the justice argument rehearsed in chapter 2—that we should be suspicious of reproductive cloning, and should refuse to countenance it unless and until we can be very sure that it will not be used in a discriminatory fashion. This places the burden of proof firmly on the would-be cloners, but like risk-benefit arguments, it stops short of an absolute prohibition.

Rights and Wrongs

I have further argued that some of the scenarios envisaged for reproductive cloning amount to the attempt to create, not merely procreate, a person. This would be tantamount to taking upon ourselves 'ultimate' tasks that properly belong to God alone: like the builders of the tower of Babel, we would be attempting to reach up to heaven and become gods. Just as the builders in the Babel story fail in their attempt, there are good reasons for thinking that we would not succeed. But just as the builders of Babel were alienated from God and from one another by their attempt to become like God, any attempt of ours to become creators would alienate us from God, who is the true source of our life and hope. I have also argued that if we attempt to take the creator's power over another human being, this will alienate us from those whom we seek to control, turning a 'Thou' into an 'It.' On these grounds, it is possible to say that the following practices (among others) would always and absolutely be wrong: cloning ourselves in an attempt to avoid the reality of our own death; cloning a dead child in order to replace him; cloning a child as a source of spare organs or tissues for a sick family member; cloning a famous or gifted individual in an attempt to replicate what she has offered to society.

The infertile couple who simply want a child may not be seeking this kind of control or power. They may not wish to become creators; the cloning may sim-

---

46   See, for example, C Clothier (chairman), *Report of the Committee on the Ethics of Gene Therapy* (London: HMSO, 1992). A notable counter-example is M Banner (chairman), *Report of the Committee to Consider the Ethical Implications of Emerging Technologies in the Breeding of Farm Animals* (London: HMSO, 1995).

ply be, as it were, a by-product of their desire for a child.[47] Regardless of their overt intentions and desires, however, there may be an implicit meaning to their action which has to do with control and the overstepping of our creaturely limits. There may, as Waters argues, be a moral structure to human parenthood that has to do with love, unconditional belonging and the recognition that our children come to us as gifts whom we are called to receive and rejoice in, not to attempt to control. This moral structure may be distorted by the practice of cloning, even if done with the most innocent and understandable of motives. Furthermore, cloning even with such innocent motives may risk what Gill calls 'procedural deterioration'—a gradual shift in practice from cloning as an exceptional last resort to a much more routine use, accompanied by a shift in attitudes from quite modest and compassionate aims towards the more pretentious and overweening tendencies that I have warned against. Taken together, these two arguments, about the implicit meaning of the practice of cloning and the risk of procedural deterioration, give us reasons for concluding at least provisionally that even the more modest and compassionate uses of reproductive cloning should not be countenanced.

The Public Debate

But what of the public policy debate? The theological arguments I have developed might be acceptable to Christians, but are they likely to impress policy-makers in a pluralist society in which the assumptions on which they are based may not be widely shared? Indeed, have Christians any *right* to try and advance their views in such a society?

The first thing to be said by way of response is that these arguments make claims about *human* flourishing. The vision embodied in these claims is, to be sure, a Christian vision, but it is a vision of what it means to be human. If Christians have any confidence in their conclusions about issues like human cloning, they have every reason to argue for those conclusions in public. But how?

Some Christians, fearing that overtly Christian theological arguments will seem incredible or unintelligible to non-Christians, favour a strategy of seeking universally-shared premises on which to build a moral argument. However, this begs the question whether there are any such universal premises—whether, as it were, there is any level moral playing-field on which Christians and others can play by rules that are fair to all. Some years ago Stanley Hauerwas, following Bernard Williams, contended that there is no such thing as 'ethics' *simpliciter*, detached from any qualifier such as 'Christian,' 'Buddhist' or 'Humanist.'[48] There may be no set of rules that favours all possible players equally.

---

47 The desire for undue control may, of course, be part of their motivation, as it may for any of us. There are many ways, even without recourse to high-tech medicine, in which parents exercise more control over their children than they have a right to, treating them more as their creatures or commodities than as gifts from God.

48 S Hauerwas, *The Peaceable Kingdom: A Primer in Christian Ethics* (London: SCM, 1984) p 18.

If so, then Christians are better advised to argue their ethical case robustly and openly as Christians. But if they do this, they need not assume that what they have to say will be of no interest to others. For one thing, in a pluralist society, policy-makers should at least theoretically take as much notice of Christian views as of those of any other minority. For another, as Michael Banner has pointed out, there is no reason why the advancement of a Christian view need not be combined with a robust critical engagement with others.[49] And Christians who are unafraid to use theological arguments in the public domain may find that their language strikes a surprisingly strong chord. The widespread use of religious language in these debates is often marked; I noted earlier *Time* magazine's use of the language of 'Xeroxing souls,' and Prince Charles is by no means the only commentator to speak in a bioethical context about 'playing God.' The use of such language may suggest a widespread, if inarticulate, recognition that these are inescapably religious questions. Even if these insights are no more than the fragmentary survivals of a Christian heritage that is rapidly disappearing from Western societies, they may encourage some openness to Christians' use of the same language. Christians who speak Christianly about such things may even win the occasional convert.

But Christian speech about bioethical questions is unlikely either to convince or to convert so long as it is only speech. The Christian churches do indeed have a responsibility to think hard and speak clearly about such matters, but they also have a third inescapable responsibility—to be communities in which the truth of what they say can be clearly seen. At the core of my argument about human cloning have been the following claims: that to be human is to be made in the image of God, which means to be in relationships that should be dialogical rather than coercive, and centred on the other rather than oneself; that parents are called to provide a place of unconditional belonging for their children, and that the structure of human parenthood is undermined by practices that call this unconditional belonging into question; and that human beings are creatures, not creators, mandated and called by God to take responsibility for 'penultimate,' but not 'ultimate,' matters. A Christian church which makes these claims has a responsibility to live by them—to be a community in which children (and others) find a place of unconditional belonging, to be a community characterized by dialogical and other-centred relationships, to live its life in humble and joyful trust in the God who is the creator and redeemer of all. If it does not show at least some signs of this way of living, its theological claims are unlikely to be taken seriously: nor should they be. As Hauerwas has said, 'The first social ethical task of the church is to be the church.'[50] That is also the beginning—though by no means the end—of the church's contribution to the human cloning debate.

49   M Banner, *Christian Ethics and Contemporary Moral Problems* (Cambridge: CUP, 1999) pp 26–40.
50   Hauerwas, *The Peaceable Kingdom*, p 99.